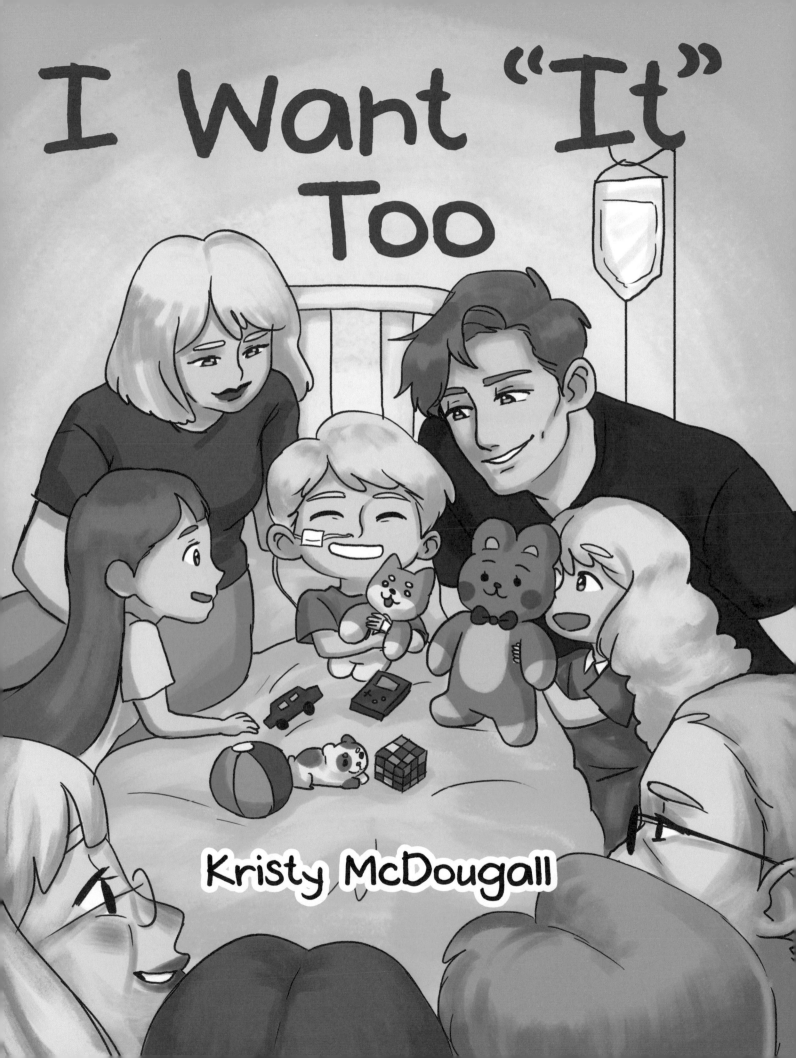

Balboa Press books may be ordered through booksellers or by contacting:

Balboa Press
A Division of Hay House
1663 Liberty Drive
Bloomington, IN 47403
www.balboapress.com.au
1 (877) 407-4847

ISBN: 978-1-5043-1887-7 (sc)
ISBN: 978-1-5043-1888-4 (e)

Print information available on the last page.

Balboa Press rev. date: 08/26/2019

BALBOA
PRESS
A DIVISION OF HAY HOUSE

I Want "It" Too

I was 6 when I first said "I want IT too."

"IT" was leukaemia (it's ok, I couldn't pronounce it either and had no idea what it was).

Is there an "IT" that has come into your family too?

What is "IT" for you? An injury from an accident or trauma? burn injury? cancer?

Or something that will take longer than a cold to recover from? That's how leukaemia was explained to me.

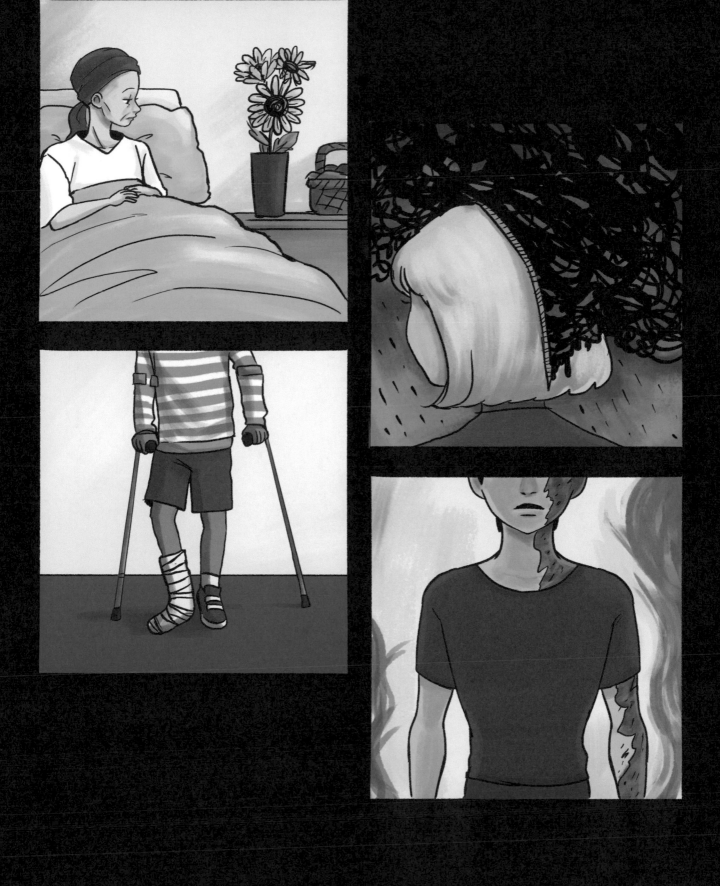

Do you want "IT" too?

When I said "I want IT too", I didn't want to be sick or in hospital with tubes hanging out of my nose, arm and foot. I didn't want to be the size of a balloon, blown up on steroids and other medications.

I just wanted the things I thought he had. Everyone bought him toys and visited him.

I wanted things back the way they were before "IT" came along. But things were never the same again.

I missed my mum and dad, when 1 or both of them were at the hospital with him. They'd sleep there too, because it was too far to come home. He was really sick.

I missed them taking me to school or picking me up.

What do you miss?

When mum and dad were both at the hospital other families looked after me. They tried to care for me. It isn't the same though as your own bed, home and family routine. Some were nice and loving. Others weren't.

I missed my room and my house. I missed sharing a room with my sister, even though I hated it when we were at home. I even missed her kicking me from the bottom bunk.

All I saw was his toys and he had all of our parent's attention.

But my world had been turned upside down too.

And this "IT" affects me too – just like it does every other member of the family too – children and adults all struggle with this new change that "IT" has caused.

Sometimes we become angry and get into trouble, when we've never been in trouble before.

Sometimes we get upset.

Sometimes we get distracted and can't focus and our previous good grades slip.

How do you feel?

We all need someone to help us with "IT."

Talk to someone you trust.

A teacher, parent, aunt, uncle, friend
and tell them how you are feeling.

Sometimes the "IT" gets better and life returns to normal and sometimes "IT" doesn't.

"IT" can take a long time.

Speak up and reach out even if it's only to 1 person, it can help with "IT."

Remember everyone else who's dealing with "IT" too. Your world isn't the only one turned upside down.

Love and support each other too.

I wish you all well and the person
with "IT" a full recovery.

Printed in the United States
By Bookmasters